Sky Mountain Trees Stars

A Collection of Short Poetry

Sky Mountain Trees Stars

A Collection of Short Poetry

by

Michael Shoemaker

Cover design by Shay Culligan
Cover image by Michael Shoemaker
Fish illustration by Viktoriya Lissachenko on Unsplash
Author photo by Michael Shoemaker

ISBN: 979-8-90146-980-4
Library of Congress Control Number: 2026938828

Kelsay Books
502 South 1040 East, A-119
American Fork, Utah 84003
Kelsaybooks.com

To my parents, Tomasene and Dennis—
the loadstars of my life.

Acknowledgments

Thank you to the following publications, in which versions of these poems previously appeared:

Autumn Moon Haiku Journal: “burning,” “quaking aspens”
The Bamboo Hut: a journal of tanshi: “skyward crows,” “man steps around man”
Cantos: A Literary and Arts Journal: “cherita”
Chrysanthemum: “twilight evening primrose”
Cold Moon Journal: “pine needle trail”
Enchanted Garden Haiku Journal: “purple and green”
Fireflies’ Light: A Magazine of Short Poems: “Wall Street hurricane,” “moving a piano up,” “an umbrella to Oregonians,” “five-pound perch story”
Haiku of the World: “morning campfire smoke”
Lothlorien Poetry Journal: “a glass, cup and bowel,” “looking back,” “lurching-to-and-fro”
Petals of Haiku: An Anthology: “robin watches,” “circling mist,” “red-tailed hawks glide” (Literary Revelations, 2024)
Presence Haiku Journal: “casting light tackle”
The Solitary Daisy: “copper-colored leaves fall”
Tranquility: An Anthology of Haiku: “morning campfire smoke,” “casting light tackle,” “—early evening,” “showering,” “waves carry out” (Literary Revelations, 2025)
Under the Bashō: “the blue heron stands”
Whispers of the Season: A Contemporary Haiku Anthology: “olive glazed siskin,” “mid-day whale watching,” “calm morning breathes” (Fresh Words, 2025)

Special thanks to Penny Horne for providing a lovely Somerset setting at the Wick Farm to write. Website: www.pennyhorne.com/accommodation.

I appreciate my fellow poet and friend, Michael Parker, for reviewing and giving skilled feedback on these poems.

Praise for *Sky Mountain Trees Stars*

Michael Shoemaker's *Sky Mountain Trees Stars* appeals to all readers, even those who aren't typical poetry fans. Though I rarely read poetry, this work enchanted me. The author's careful word choice delivers a range of effects; some poems made me chuckle, while others gave me pause. The Christian haiku can inspire and deepen one's time in God's word. Shoemaker's nature poems evoke vivid images. Clear explanations of the book's poetry forms helped me appreciate each style. This book is a refreshing read for all. Even busy readers can fit in a short poem. I, however, read it in one sitting and plan to return to it.

—Alice H. Murray, award-winning author, writer, reporter, & editor of *Go! Christian Magazine*

Haiku, in the hands of a skillful writer, is a painting that says a thousand words. Michael Shoemaker is more than a skillful writer. He is an observer of the world around him. And given three short lines with which to work, he draws you into the world he sees . . . one of beauty, depth, and nuance.

Senryū, tanka, cherita, and cinquain are also brandished. Michael is a passionate master of all short-form poetry. He captures a scene, conveys a story, and brings the world to life—all by pointing out a few select details that others would simply overlook. *Sky Mountain Trees Stars* is a remarkable collection to be enjoyed by all lovers of poetry!

—Christopher A. Hostettler, poet & author, *Tales of the Captain*

Contents

Haiku	13
Christian Haiku	23
Haiku of Place	29
Seasonal Haiku	32
Senryū	49
Tanka	57
Cherita	65
Sijo	75
American or Adelaide Crapsey Cinquains	81
Dyadic Cinquains	85
Standard Cinquains ABABB Rhyming Scheme	89
Oh, How I Need Thee	93

Haiku

casting light tackle
high into the wind above
crashing sounds of surf

morning campfire smoke
curls and rises above pines
meadowlark's singsong

twilight evening primrose rises with the North Star

purple and green
clover and violets
color in stone walls

quaking aspens
spinning leaves
into daydreams

skyward crows
pine needles spiraling
into my hand

showering
peach blossoms
make sneakers sing

pink lemonade flamingos
spear the orange sky
drawing colors upward

pine needle trail
draws me back
to hidden childhood hollows

hidalgo Don Quixote
pirouettes, not piercing
windmills of imagination

between clothes baskets
crouching leaning forward cat
ready to ambush

twilight evening primrose rises with the North Star

healthy greenest kale
creeps down my throat ending with
a slithering gag

on holiday
no work security badge
something missing

arch of my life
window to my soul
prospect through your love

garden rain catcher
silent tear carrier
thanks, Peruvian lily

too nervous to cook
lime Slurpees and pizza
first week at college

la mer Debussy
what I hear when I put my ear
to a seashell

a truck careens
to a fiery destruction
indeliberate words

sonorous wind chimes
evensong from the abbey
prayers for long calm sleep

angel pirouettes in the snow—heartache defense

Christian Haiku

All scriptural references are taken from the Authorized King James Version of the Bible. I invite you to read along in whatever version of the Bible that is part of your scripture study.

I hope that any version you refer to in your study will amplify the inspired truth and beauty felt and understood through these haiku pieces.

dove of peace
rising sun prayer
uplifting comfort

these gaping wounds healed
void's saving nail prints
tomb portal safety now

James 1:27

pure religion
visit the fatherless
alienated

blessed are those who
receive some relief than
no relief at all

Nehemiah 9:17

slow to anger
ready to pardon
Captain of my soul

Psalms 119:105

early morn scriptures
and hymns—lamp to my feet
light unto my path

teaching reading
can open
the gates to Zion

mothers outlast
angels' love and have to be
twice as quick

fathers
tools of irrelevance
say demons

Corinthians 13:8

charity never faileth
but we do sometimes
forgiveness makes us clean

shot dead stole his boots
ancestor's faithful martyrdom
leads the righteous charge

God is exalted
above fruitful field and peak
sing praise and glory

Haiku of Place

—Hyde Park, London
steeped tea and clouds
genie wish rug scrolls

the Waving Girl smiles
pink magnolias unfold
—Savannah's river street

no lions and bears
Piccadilly Circus night stop
bridesmaids' party alights

Oxford station call
missing Valencia oranges'
sweet nectar

Cartwright Gardens bench
the sway and sigh of high leaves
tennis balls hop at play

some public British
gardens have gates padlocks
chains-free the butterflies

Magdalen college
green grass imprints on elbows
robins learn from worms

Serpentine lake
dream of riviera cruise
paddle the boat more

London—Exeter
railway line follows sunset
and skein of geese home

Seasonal Haiku

fall

burning
autumn leaves
loneliness

hurricane force
sirens left blaring
hope pancaked

turquoise sardine clouds
baked red furrows hide weeds
sense heaven

monarch butterflies rise to a falling leaf occasion

Thanksgiving
a reason to sit
a purpose to kneel

fallen eucalyptus
leaves-to whom I
shed my tales

menagerie calm
stars gas dust gravity bound
Milky Way in order

slow café sounds
water beads on cool glass
then runs—autumn rain

stubble fields
no untelling
that I must go on

sturdy sustenance
porridge noodles pancakes
crepes gluten-free buckwheat

olive glazed siskin
meek of the earth lullaby
alight autumn moor

migrating storks
passing through the Strait of Gibraltar
goodness that raises heads

winter

hoar-frosted pine trees
soldiers' silhouettes
against silver falls

red-tailed hawks glide
snowflakes rise
to vaulted plateaus

first Christmas day
when Manna came down to save
dwell Emmanuel

mid-day whale watching
breaching arches rise to reach
spiraling rainbows

swirling pear wassail spices
din in the orchard
Twelfth Night

falconer shades eyes raises limb then swoosh and away

pioneer quilt
faith and calm
ancestors' gift

digging for treasure
found a missed turnip
roast with honey glaze

November's first snow
picking winter quince dulce
de membrillo

codfish
a looker only
to the horrified

bean soup again
our favorite meal
please pass Tabasco

spring

robin watches
me unearth
last year's beets

azaleas
bring raindrops
lifting my spirits

circling mist
bathe hanging moss
distilling peace

to willows only
I whisper
love secrets

spring fed cottonwoods
hot yellow lightning
rain burst claps

California poppy
in baking—cooking oil
spices and superbloom

let me take my
magic wand to float upon
soap bubbles

Palm Sunday
Blessed is the King of Israel
Michael's best friend

asparagus sprouts cut
catfish caught for survival
of my dad—Stockton channels

crocus mom's favorite
maybe because it rhymes with
hocus—she liked magic

flying squirrel
Creator’s way to say, “Look
up once in a while.”

I imitate
windmill arms
dizzy must sit down

the chirp-click of nightingale’s nocturne rings true through
the woods

summer

ocean winds' fingers
trace playful shapes in the sand
stirring gulls and dunes

billowing tall clouds
rumble across the valley
cold drops pelt my skin

months of chill and frost
to plan summer festival
neighbors' laughter warmth

calm morning breathes in
emerald water meadow
quail bolting skyward

sky tosses
salad of color upswept
beyond reach

hollyhocks so tall
submit to sun bleached winds
garden's purple heart

swimming pool sizzles
last cannonball plunge
—summer's revenge

morning glories wind
cling fervently tight
—my trust in you

if I swallowed
a firefly would it
light a path within

—wisteria
honey bees’
sweet nectar of delight

Senryū

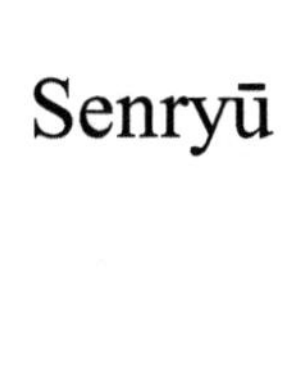

man steps around man
on sidewalk to watch opera
about suffering

moving a piano up
to the fourteenth floor
a test of friendship

mom plays tag
catches love

—five-pound perch story
uncle tells again
with smiling eyes

Wall Street hurricane
stalled by talk
of impenetrable ice

paycheck is light
bills are heavy
—fantasy book escape

a glass, cup, and bowl
can hold back
a flood in the desert

—tick tock dreams
the sound of life
running out the clock

boss states new policy
workers' ears aghast
myths, fibs and fairy tales

raising an arm high
mirrors elephant lifting trunk
watching me

—new soft puppies
giggles
engulf hearts

exercise gym hat
McDonald’s bag Starbuck cup
could it make sense

meditation garden
fractured pieces into one
til the trash truck comes

quiet coach
Great Western Railway Oxford
backpack zippers roar

baby buggy
e-scooter—don’t consider
the possibilities

beetle on pool cover
magic disappearing act
yikes! check swimsuit

I shaved by sight
now by feel—let me know
when stubble speaks

dalmatian running
partner where I always
am falling behind

Tanka

lurching to-and-fro
prow dissects grey ocean waves
lifts bubbling white foam
rises cool salty fragrance
as if from some sea flower

under the oak tree
our searching fingers reach out
leaves tumble freely
on one side apology
on the other forgiveness

Brazilian blue bliss
from hot savannah rise these
squealing screechers then
land so near me peering through
whited eye rings warily

archeologists
pass through clandestine arches
of sandstone to seek
what I see in the mirror
shaving conscientiously

hail pounds with fervor
covering all other noise
rattling windowpanes
the pastor preaches with power
and love to move human hearts

handcrafted hope chest
filled with dreams and potpourri
herbs, flowers, sweet spices
enough to combat
the rising tide of disbelief

used can opener
rings the lid freeing tangy
salt air and screech of
gulls rimming wavelength betwixt
my tongue and Yuki's whiskers

contrails lance sky
mauve mountain peaks
descending mists kiss
copper riverbed roiling sands
thunderclaps snap

crawling red eye flight
Wyoming drags it out
Nebraska pushes back
South Dakota pulls
all on a digital map

sulfur dioxide
cabbage smell fireworks
plug nose—open eyes
pop bang bomb—pungent savor
a smile can fire our souls

wrens scabble tile eaves
see-through daytime moon transfixed
swimming in Penny's pool
wakes of premillennial
paradisiacal glories

little owls hoot
in the bursting plum orchard
bees halo vervain
I find a mallard feather
and honk honk into sunset's arms

with one accord we
sing a simple hymn of praise
what is basic when
we worship the King of Kings
God of All arrayed in white

for homeless free food
not fallen from a tree, but
bought from dolls, kids' bikes,
bus pass instead of walking
opener needed for cans

John 14:18

old church closed today
no more services
new social center
I will not leave you comfortless:
I will come unto you.

diabetes
injections, pills, tiredness
Glad to be alive,
sad to be ill, stupid
awkward waiting room.

bumblebees rumble
in the center of the bass
banjo picks me up
along Smokey Mountain train tracks
fiddler falling in with leaves

By 2050
NASA aims for a moon base
and a trip to Mars.
I hope to make it through snarled
traffic to buy/afford meds.

Cherita

crack then rolling thunder rumbles

hailstorm beats the steel carport
we sit safe in the barn's sweet-smelling hay

recalling how scared and nervous we were to graduate
and how not all has changed that much
except we now hold hands and look straight in each other's
eyes

the inconsistencies of poverty

cough without a doctor
relocation without a home

moons without a job
hunger without future promise
spirit barely hanging on—time ticking

four-wing saltbush

apothecary of Southwest sand dunes
poultice for ant bites

part of alkaline solution
to remove pericarp of maize
for hominy, tortillas, and tamales

June 2030, Paddington Station

backpacker ready and balanced
right foot forward and left foot back, resting easy

terminal display appears
blinks once and steps forward
destination—2090, Mars Station via moon

We watched cartoons on Saturday morning.

Commercials pumped the air brakes on fun,
but we loved used car salesman, Cal Worthington.

We cheered as walked out with his “dog” Spot which
sometimes was a zebra, orangutan or elephant.
How did you know all the boys on my street couldn’t pay to
go to the zoo? Thanks Cal.

No sabes nada

tenéis que aprender
orejas de burro
se van a crecer

una canto de amor y sabiduría
cantado a misioneros por niños risueños
de la calle Argentinos

Translation:

You don't know anything.

You need to learn.
You have donkey ears
that will grow.

A chant of love and wisdom
sung to missionaries by laughing
Argentine street children.

Cincinnati Reds Stadium

stretched and caught a foul ball one-handed
Chicago dog in the other

the stinging and pulsating hand
makes it easy to confess to
my doctor I am still alive

When I read . . .

Taunton, UK Flower Show is back for its 194th year
I asked why every town doesn't have a flower show?

If we had more flower shows
would we need as many
war memorials?

A small almost secretive never landing white butterfly

filled with garden schemes over the hedge
at one moment here, next flitting anywhere

past the spicy vanilla of rugosa roses
thru blue Love-in-a-mist, golden pots of marigold, creme dahlias, pink yarrow and Sneezewort (which I could not makeup) to at last land on the tip of your pinkie ring finger.

NASA's Artemis III mission seems more long shot
than moonshot.

The first plan to walk on the moon since 1972
is beleaguered and delayed.

Heat shield and life support system issues moved dates back. Starship HLS lunar lander trials failed five out of nine times. Budget cuts are coming. Forty to fifty percent of lunar missions fail. Ground Control to Major Tom and drifting.

My sweet land of liberty

land of my birth, water and blood,
home and defense of all natural rights.

I vote freely guided by conscience.
You may speak your mind.
The Constitution and Bill of Rights lead the way.

crack then rolling thunder rumbles

hailstorm beats the steel carport
we sit safe in the barn’s sweet-smelling hay

recalling how scared and nervous we were to graduate
and how not all has changed that much
except we now hold hands and look straight in each other’s
eyes

Sijo

Once more, into the deep

A blind marine biologist
    receives a terse notice,
"I'm sorry ma'am, guide dogs
    are not allowed in the restaurant,"
and here she thought sharks and
    giant octopodes the only things to fear.

Alladale Wilderness Reserve—Scottish Highlands

What once was will be again.
Only one percent of wild woods left.
They come back almost two by two
pine martens, eagles, red deer, wildcats.
Rowan, birch, pine, a million replanted.
Embrace the saplings.

"In the Twilight" by: Sir Arnold Bax, Ulster Orchestra

Strings release blue mist and chill
    over the downhill slope to home.
Horns stand alone surveying
    vast interludes from a peak.
Flutes raise sunset thrush song
    to attic bedroom chamber prayer.

Working Graveyard at the Emergency Room

While most people sleep
the E.R. impels or wanes, receiving
from paramedics, ambulances
and walk-ins;
when a nurse yells down the hall,
"You're nothing, but a filthy drunk."

Clouds for Wimbledon

A friend arrives late from the pub
    saying they hope for clouds.
Watching ice lollies drip and drain
    with a slurp on Centre Court
ball boys and girls gain fresh bravado
    to cross superheated space.

Clouds for Sudan

Rain from June to September clouds
    is vital for crops and animals,
drinking and irrigation water.
    Who will remain to see them?
With a going civil war,
    three million have fled and more daily.

Clouds for Ethan

He got a job at a store and
    told them of epilepsy
he couldn't work night shifts.
    They scheduled him anyway.
After three seizures he missed
    the next shift and was fired.

Artist Residency—Wick Farm—near Langport, UK

Buzzards and seagulls sailing mates
    uprising on the morning guided breeze.
I propel backstroke through
    tea-coulored sea water pool
a monarch butterfly escapes the vegetable
    garden kissing dawn.

American or Adelaide Crapsey Cinquains

Neighborhood Food Pantry Finds

fennel,
cloves, paprika
canned candied yams and gourds.
"What are these and what can we make?"
"Search me."

Question to an F-15 Eagle Pilot

What do
you think in a
crystalline shell going
a thousand miles per hour? blue
side up.

The Good Spies' Report

Numbers chapters 13 and 14

grapes, figs,
pomegranates,
a land that flows with
milk and honey, if we delight
the Lord.

Finger vs. Pick

What can
you call something
that doesn’t feel old and
doesn’t feel new? Eternity
strumming?

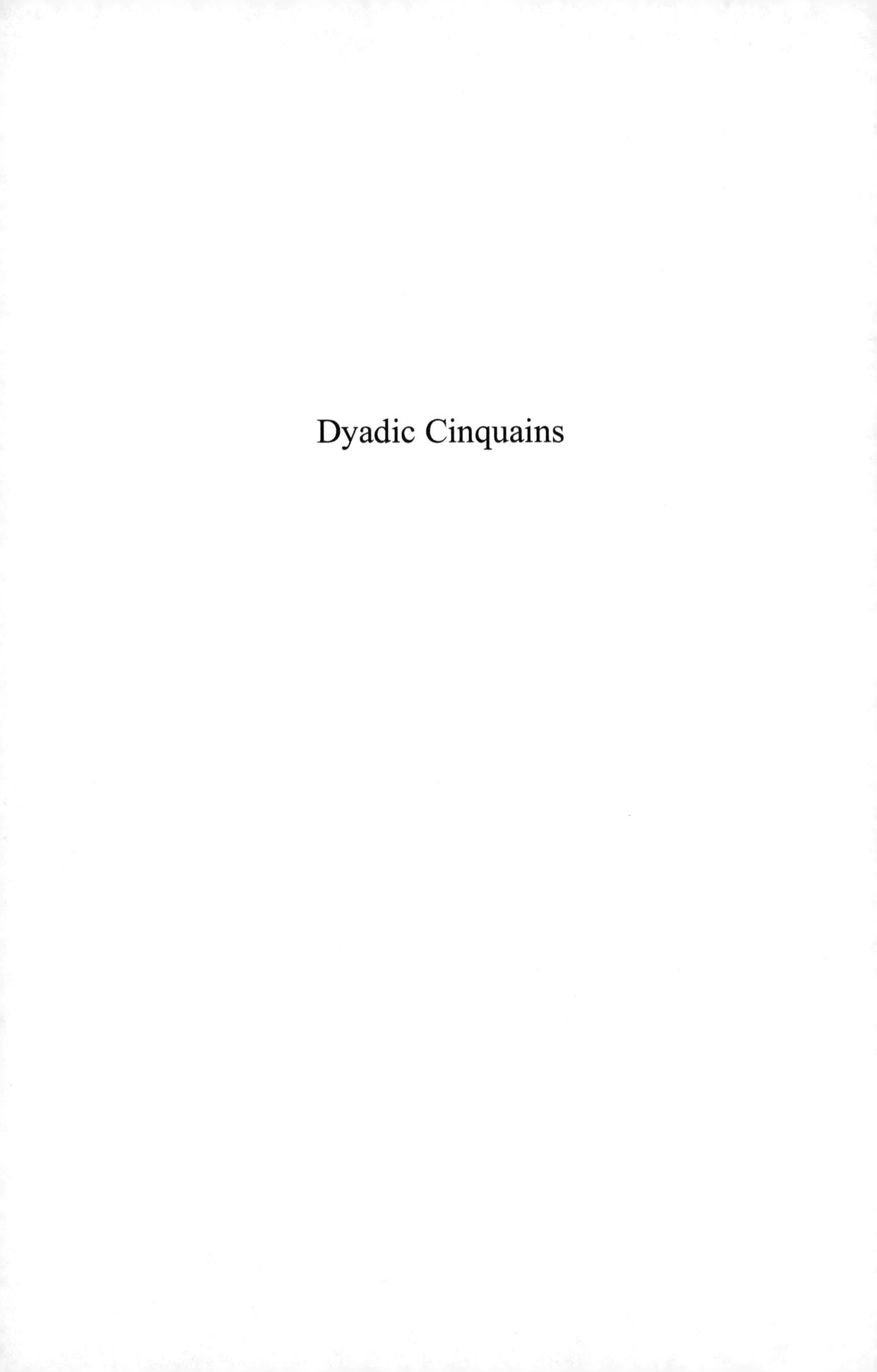

Dyadic Cinquains

February Thaw

Icicles
shining, translucent
drip making pools
expelling cats from under
window sills.

Edison Street—Silent Movies—Salt Lake City

oohgaah!
honking, blaring
organ-made car horn
Blaine Gale amuses moviegoers
golden

Independence Day-July 4th

Liberty
expansive, soul-serving
kneeling to pray
standing up to speak
duty

They say they come to save democracy

Deception
insidious, power-grasping
deal making reprobates
choking the peoples' voice
guard

Up All January Night

Words
time-traveling, space-spanning
leaving me wakeful
scanning the ceiling for
spiders

Standard Cinquains
ABABB Rhyming Scheme

Apple Valley, California

Most people flow by the place of my birth
going south while the river glistens north
seen as a bypass, not unlike our earth.
Some may find the desert salt landscape course.
It is the elegant gait of a horse.

In the Name of Business

In ancient Rome slavery was known well
from houses to farms to mines you would see
oft masters' whips and brands to compel
and now in cruel bonds identically
"trafficking" it's called without dignity.

If Killed at Antietam . . .

In battlefield broken, men fell in mass
hastily laid in shallow unmarked graves;
then reinterred in dedicated grass.
When computer keystroke command behaves
nonbeing comes on anonymous waves.

Saturday Drives

After the divorce it was mom and I.
“Work before play” so chores were done by noon.
Then off on Oregon backroads rain or dry.
A spread of cheese and crackers was our tune.
When love is laugh and listen, joys’ balloons.

When Came We Unto Thee? Matthew 25:39

Oftentimes a half wrong feels full in bloom
when a minister loves the people true,
but hates hospital and prison perfume.
It’s when you’ll see from what wood you are hew
to travel in faith where Jesus is too.

Oh, How I Need Thee

Help of the helpless, Lord. Do not know how to speed up the healing of scars on my left knee from a bike accident. Unsure how to advise a friend on how to find a better job. What is going on that my car's engine service light is coming on again? Where should I take it in to get it checked? I wonder why these tomato plants aren't sprouting. Is it too hot, windy or dry or is it just my inattention in caring for them?

Should a supervisor call out and make fun of a co-worker in front of others? What can I do about it, if anything? Why do I keep on losing my temper again, again, and as You know, again, when it is the last thing that I want to do? I hope this seventy-times-seven thing is really working. I thought by my age I would be wiser, kinder and gentler, yet I wonder why so often it doesn't appear to be working out that way. What can I do to help the poor when their daily calls for help threaten to engulf me? How can I help them if I am not always well? What can I do with the sorrow I feel over losing wild places of reflection, animals, plants, water and air? Will Isaiah's prophecy of the desert blooming as a rose come to pass? What do I need to do so I don't tire of the desert and move out before Christ comes again? Refresh, oh refresh me, Dear Father.

Do I need to worry about pruning those future rose bushes now? Don't know how to help family members who are far and away. No guesses left of how to stop wars, hate and famine in this multiple spinning-plate world of ours.

How well You listen to what my heart says: words can't express and lips can't form!

I bring these to Thee. You know all things. Help of the helpless, Lord, abide with me.
Peaceful Presence is power enough.

Because of Thee, I've got Love like an ocean in my soul.

Imperfect prayers are not ineffectual.
They move the mightiest of mountains.

About the Author

Michael Shoemaker was raised in Southern California. He earned a Bachelor's of Science degree in Psychology from Brigham Young University in Provo, Utah, and a Master's of Arts degree in Marriage and Family Therapy from Pacific Lutheran University in Tacoma, Washington. He has served Utahans in the field of Vocational Rehabilitation for 26 years. Michael is happily married to Tamary Shoemaker and is the father of three adult children.

Michael served a mission for The Church of Jesus Christ of Latter-day Saints in Argentina and is a temple ordinance worker in the Taylorsville Utah Temple. He relies on Jesus's mercy and grace to change every day.

Michael is a poet, haikuist, writer, photographer, and editor from Magna, Utah where he lives with his wife and son. He enjoys hiking in the canyons of Wasatch Mountains and exploring the natural wonders of Southern Utah.

He is the author of *Rocky Mountain Reflections, Grasshoppers in the Field* and *Sacred Strains of Praise,* three poetry/photography collections.

His Japanese and Korean short-form poetry has appeared in *Haiku Commentary, Presence Haiku Journal, Enchanted Garden Haiku Journal, Scarlet Dragonfly Journal, Sea-shores Haiku Journal, Cold Moon Journal, Bamboo Hut: a journal of tanshi, The Solitary Daisy, Fireflies' Light: A*

Journal of Short Poetry, Under the Bashō, Chrysanthemum, Lothlorien Poetry Journal, Haiku of the World, Autumn Moon Haiku Journal, The Pan Haiku Review, and *Inkpot Literary Journal.* Michael is as an Editorial Consultant for *Cantos: A Literary and Arts Journal* and Michael serves on the board of the Utah State Poetry Society as Historian/ Librarian.

Michael has been writing since childhood, but started publishing in 2023. Since then, his work has been published in journals and magazines 150 times and appears in 32 anthologies.

International recognition includes the publication of his poetry in *Boundless 2026, Boundless 2025, Boundless 2024: The Anthology of the Rio Grande Valley International Poetry Festival, Petals of Haiku: An Anthology,* and *Tranquility: An Anthology of Haiku* which were haiku anthologies that were #1 top Amazon Releases. Three of Michael's poems have been short listed for The Letter Review Prize for Poetry. He is a three-time nominee for the Best of the Net Anthology awards and for a Pushcart Prize Award. Michael received an honorable mention in the Writer's Digest 94th Annual Competition.

He creates to uplift and delight others and share beauty, truth, loveliness, purity and human connectedness. With so many people worldwide living in isolation Michael wants to help others to connect with others and the world around them. He is excited for the future and firmly believes that the best is yet to come.

www.ingramcontent.com/pod-product-compliance
Lightning Source LLC
LaVergne TN
LVHW020651100826
845148LV00012B/2433

* 9 7 9 8 9 0 1 4 6 9 8 0 4 *